# From Longing To *Forever*

Meherpreet Kaur

# DEDICATION

To everyone who professed love and taught me to love every day.

And to my lucky charm, who always supports me and loves me.

# From Longing to Forever

Love isn't just a word—it's more than four letters.

Within these four letters lie seven stages.

It is surrender, a quiet offering of the self.

It is questions wrapped in beauty.

Uncertain, yet ever-transforming.

A haven, a refuge, a home.

A game of faith and patience.

Master it, and it is yours to keep.

Meherpreet Kaur

# ATTRACTION

# 1.

The very first stage seems to hold ten letters,
Yet, it is more than just a handful of letters.

The way, on a random Saturday,
A random someone becomes more than someone.
The way you begin to admire them,
The way you wish to carry their scent
Everywhere you stand.

The way a pair of random eyes
They seem made to be stared at—just stared.
The way all their imperfections
Melt into effortless perfection.
The way all you can do is wonder,
"How are they so perfect?"

That's the feeling you're scared to feel.
For in the end,
It may be pleasing, maybe heart-wrenching,
Maybe compelling may be uncontrollable,
Maybe Uncertain, yet metamorphic.

And yet, you stay still,
Adoring—ignoring—
The confusion inherited
All on a random Saturday.

# 2.

I stared out the window,
Gazing upon an astonishing view—
A view of them.

And I admired them with every passing second,
I wished they would admire me too.

Then, in an instant,
Our eyes met, intertwining,
Gazing deep into each other's souls
Through the brown of our eyeballs.

And in that moment,
I learned that perhaps,
I had thoughtlessly allowed myself
To fall, unknowingly,
Into the attraction for someone.

# 3.

There are many selenophiles,
Professing love for the moon's gentle gleam.
I am one of them.

Yet, some of us overlook its quiet wonders—
The way it lingers between dark clouds,
Weaving its glow into their embrace.

I adore how its pale light spills into a rainbow,
Bringing colour to the black and white.

And as I stand here, lost in admiration,
I realise this view feels familiar.

To be a selenophile, to be someone's moon,
To be seen, to be cherished,
To be lost in the way they admire my beauty—
Unaware that their gaze alone
Turning my black and white into
A rainbow dancing amidst the clouds

## 4.

Attraction—it starts so simple,
Yet stirs a world we never knew.
A glance, a voice, a fleeting moment,
Unheard, unseen—yet felt so true.

A stranger, distant, yet so striking,
It becomes the thought we can't let go of.
A silent pull, a quiet longing,
A spark that sets the heart aglow.

We praise their smallest triumphs softly,
Cherish words they never hear.
Drawn toward their world so gently,
Finding joy just standing near.

A fleeting force, yet all-consuming,
So light, so sweet—yet ever blood

From Longing to Forever

# ATTACHMENT

# 1.

Attachment—ten letters, another phase,
Something so magical, so surreal,
You wonder if what you feel is real.

The moments just before love's flight,
A phase that fills your heart with plight.
You question how you question why—
Someone you feel you've known for years gone by,
Now sees your soul, beyond disguise,
Knows you more than your own eyes.

It startles you yet draws you in,
A silent pull, a whispered spin.
You let them learn, you let them trace
The hidden thoughts you once encased.
And so, you stand—no fear, no guise,
Letting them read you through their eyes.

## 2.

One day,
You'd have no interest in knowing someone,
Nor is letting them know you.

But then, on some random day,
You'd both click over a passing joke.
And somehow, they'd come to know
The smallest details about you—
And you, about them.

You'd talk,
Forgetting when you shared your likes and dislikes,
Yet they'd remember it all.

They'd know when you're sad,
When you're mad,
When you're happy,
When you're wild,
When you're crying,
And when excitement lights up your eyes.

And in their knowing,
You'd feel as if they've known you
For more than just a lifetime.

## 3.

On a night when you weep being unseen,
They sense it—hidden in your texts.
You're stunned, yet not ready to speak,
While they sit on the other end,
Patiently wait to hear.

With quiet resistance, you begin to speak,
And as the trembling words spill, so do your tears.
And somehow, with every sentence,
You tend to feel lighter and lighter.

This moment, unseen yet deeply felt,
Reveals how, without wanting to,
You've grown attached—
A bond is woven in deep, unspoken, powerful
understanding,
Stitched together in shared words.

# 4.

On a random day, my friend mentioned,
"Their presence makes your day."
I replied—

Perhaps my day begins in despair,
With disbelief, with doubtful faith.
Perhaps I am exhausted, hopeless, lost,
Yet their existence breathes life into me.

Their smile makes my lips smile,
Their presence soothes my restless heart.
Their patience embraces my bizarreness,
Their gaze finds beauty in my being.
They cherish the madness in me,
And in my joy, they find their joy.
With gentle words, they lead the way for my wrongs,
Turning sorrow into something soft, something bright.

So I seek them—
In my morning, my noon, and my night

# 5.

Attachment- a word that carries so much within.
A phase that leads to something beautiful.

When all your thoughts circle them,
When all your thoughts begin only to let their name
linger on your lips,
When they are all you talk to, all you talk about.
When you tend to wonder—are you falling?

The universe whispers in signs,
Drawing you closer, hints by hints, line by line.
And that is when you may know—
You've moved beyond mere attachment.

# LOVE

# 1.

Love—a phase, a pleasing one.
Something that lights up your soul.

For some, it's the slightest of efforts,
For others, it's how they feel: happy, lucky, lively, thrilled,
or cheerful.
For some, it's haven; for others, it's magic.

Love is the most powerful sorcery to exist.
It can change, raise, and grow the unexpected,
It can even heal the deepest traumas.

Love is bound to happen.
It then doesn't matter if it's a stranger, an enemy, a friend,
Or even someone you no longer speak to.
It also doesn't matter if you don't believe in it.

Love is the language of Oneness.
Love is the language of Hearts.
Love is the language of the Universe.
Love is indeed one soul in two different bodies.

## 2.

You won't recall the moment you first felt drawn to
them,
Nor the instant your heart grew attached.
All you'll know is—you fell.

You'll remember how they feel like home,
How, in their presence, you were never alone.
You'll both know you are meant to be,
Yet all you'll give each other are subtle yet obvious
hints.
You'll prefer lingering in each other's worlds,
inseparable.
But no one will dare to confess.

Perhaps you'll talk for hours,
And they'll listen, memorizing every word.
Perhaps, when no one's watching, they'll steal glances,
Admiring you from afar, tracing your nickname as their
girl.
Perhaps you'll laugh at the silliest things; they do
Unknowing, it's love in soft displays.
Perhaps, you both already recognize—
Still, wait for a time more perfect than now,
Unaware that this moment, this love is just right.

## 3.

On a random day,
As you talk to them,
They'll tell you how they knew—
Knew you were the one,
The name, your name, carved beside theirs
In the book of Lovers.

They'll speak of the signs you both ignored,
How destiny whispered while you turned away.
How you found them—your saviour—
A moment they remember vividly,
Though you search your mind a thousand times,
Try to look for it in your memory.

In a time of distance, when even small talk died,
They'll recall, one day, a message they sent,
And suddenly, a bond grew.
They'll so continue and bring out,
More signs, more whispers that were left unnoticed
But this time, these signs were shining clear in
remembrance.
Yet now, as you listen, as you think
It feels as if the universe,
Perhaps, just perhaps—
Has written both of your names as
Two lovers, side by side,
Inscribed forever in the book of Lovers.

# 4.

There's a string—
A red string, they say.
A thread that binds two soul mates,
Invisible and everlasting thread of fate
Perhaps you believed it,
Or perhaps you pondered—
Who stands at the other end of your red string?

They say this thread never snaps,
Yet the one you assumed held the other end—
They broke.

However, you then found someone.
But, unknowingly, you drifted apart,
Unknowingly, you disregarded destiny's whisper.
Yet, the string did not break—
It solely tangled, waiting for them all over again.
And then, fate wove you together once more,
As the red string slowly untwined.
Your faith in the red string grew stronger,
Leading you back—
To them, the one you had yearned for all along.

## 5.

You may see a couple,
And in their presence, you'll be reminded of them.
You'll notice how their gaze potters,
Always around you, wrapped in your stories.
And as you walk, like the lovers you saw,
They'll stumble—
Lost in you, forgetting the world.

In that moment, you'll anticipate
The way they make you feel at home, a haven.
You'll ponder—
How they call you by your nickname, so clear, so warm.
How they listen to your gossip, their laughter a timeless
tale of love.
How they scold, yet mend, like a lover, a guide, a
dearest friend in one.
How they see the child within you—honour-bound and
brave.
How they wipe veiled tears, silencing hidden fears.
How they love with all their might,
Turning darkness into light.

And all of this, together, makes your soul believe—
That this love is just right,
Where two souls are bound by an unseen string,
And their names are carved forever in the Book of
Lovers.

# TRUST

## 1.

Trust- a word of just five letters
Still, more than a word, its meaning liberates.

Trust is the pillar leading to forever.
At this stage, love nurtures trust,
Causing, two souls to unite, reserving two hearts, and
intensifying love.

From whispered words to hearts laid bare
From quiet glances to the old tales we share
From limitless secrets to moments of grandeur.

And bit by bit, this five-letter word nurtured by both,
Writes a fairy tale, all written by you.

## 2.

On a random night,
While you'll lay on your bed, trying to fall asleep.
You'll realise how building trust between you and them,
Never really asked for a second thought.

Despite the time of distance, when small talk faded,
Despite your trust issues,
You never waited; you simply trusted them.
You innocently shared all your problems with them.

You ponder more into it and realise maybe because-
You found love balanced with them when you felt your
heart heavy.
You saw the heroism in the way they made you feel
when all you could feel was despair.
You think of the faith, how it kept whispering while
you simply ignored it.

All of this pondering couldn't answer why you never
thought again,
But, thinking about the art of Trust between you,
You'll feel calm and at peace, easily falling asleep.

Meherpreet Kaur

# WORSHIP

# 1.

Very close to the final stage.
There is a stage, a stage known as Worship.
It's exactly what the word itself sounds like.

It's like a conch reverberating before the god.
It is them, your idols,
As you praise the deeds, they are carved deep inside
your core.

It's you, circling the Prayer plate around them,
Discerning them as your deity.

It's you, singing their name in endless devotion—
Like Mirabai of this new generation.

It is you, Raidas, devoted to their God,
Crafting them in the light to your clay lamp, the pearl to
your thread of being.

It's you who worships them,
Making love even bolder.

## 2.

Worship—something you've been lingering upon.
And so, you'll perceive that,
Everything you do for them, to them, or about them,
Becomes a ritual offered to the divine.

You'll understand—
How you remember the smallest details,
But now, as if lighting a candle in reverence.

You will realize—
That the way you love, the way you praise,
Is like singing hymns for your deity in devotion.

You will know—
The way you stand in awe, the way you gaze, the way
you think about them in their absence,
Is the disciple in you, deliberately offering, honouring,
their extraordinariness in your life.

And then this will illuminate the celebration of your
beloved
Transforming love into a sacred shine.
Turning mundane into something divine.

## 3.

Worshipping your beloved results in
Transforming love into a sacred shine,
Turning mundane into something divine

"But how does worshipping your beloved make a
difference?"
A random thought—perhaps you'll comprehend this.

And then, you'll understand—
You love them,
But in a way where,
You surrender yourself,
As if love itself is an act of worship.

You'll notice—
You feel free to trust them,
You'll share your thoughts, emotions without any
hesitation.
You do this because you are devoted—
You are surrendered to them, to your deity.

And, while you worship,
While you give yourself away for them,
You'll realize—
This stage has drawn you closer to your beloved,
Just before the painful Death.

Meherpreet Kaur

# DEATH

# 1.

This is the final stage— Death.
A stage that seems painful,
Yet holds a quiet beauty.

Here, you must leave the world.
You may go, but they may not—
And that is the twist.
You depart this life,
Only to wait for them
In a world beyond

However, there's another fate—
One where you're fortunate,
To step beyond this loop together

Countless paths may lay before,
But in the end, you find—
The actual peace, the actual home, the actual heaven,
All with them.

## 2.

Death is a stage where—
You wait patiently, just for them to join you beyond the
loop.
It is when you compare them in the real world and the
parallel—
Yet, all you see is their angelic beauty,
Even in the world beyond.

In this parallel realm, you live thousands of more
moments just with them.
You'll feel the same spark, the same beginning,
But this time, where death is inevitable.
Where time is stretched like an endless thread,
Until the first gaze feels like living again.
You'll trust them more than ever,
Ending up telling even the things buried deep hidden in
your soul.

Perhaps, meeting again will take time,
Or perhaps, you may never meet at all,
But the red string woven in the real world,
It will bind the two souls even across dimensions.
Perhaps you'll gaze again— not out of the window,
But you'll gaze, simply to admire them, as they once
admired you.

This won't leave any mark on the body,
But, it will bring peace to the soul,
The type of peace a living being only dream of.
For in the quiet parallel world,
Two souls remain,
Their names still engraved bounded beyond time.

# Gratitude

Thank You reader! I hope you enjoyed the book the way I enjoyed writing it.

I assume, you enjoyed reading it and so, I'd recommend you to hit Instagram and check out my page and follow. You can even leave your reviews in my DMs or post about this book tagging me so that I can acknowledge you as an amazing reader and an amazing person who gave a try to a new author. You can also recommend ideas you'd like me to write on and I might execute your ideas in my own format.

Instagram handle– @meherpreettt._.kaur